Fatima & the Immaculate Heart of Mary

Celebrating the First Five Saturdays

by

Fr Anton Nadrah OCist

All booklets are published thanks to the generous support of the members of the Catholic Truth Society

CATHOLIC TRUTH SOCIETY
PUBLISHERS TO THE HOLY SEE

Contents

 First published 2016 by The Incorporated Catholic Truth Society, 40-46 Harleyford Road, London SE11 5AY Tel: 020 7640 0042 Fax: 020 7640 0046.

ISBN 978 1 78469 125 7

Originally published in Slovenian as Pet Prvih Sobot *by Salve Publishers, Ljubljana, Slovenia 2012*

Preface

In 2017, one hundred years will have passed since the Virgin Mary appeared six times to three shepherd children in Fatima, Portugal, during World War I. These little shepherds were Lucia dos Santos, ten, her cousin Francisco Marto, nine, and his little sister Jacinta, seven. The Virgin Mary invited them to pray and do penance for peace and the conversion of sinners and to live a faithful life according to the Gospel. When Pope Benedict XVI went to Portugal in May 2010, he stressed that the aim of Fatima is "continuous conversion, penance, prayer and the three theological virtues, faith, hope and charity". These messages stressed the devotion to the Immaculate Heart of Mary which culminates in the consecration to her Heart. One year previously the shepherds had been addressed by the Angel of Peace. He taught them two prayers and prepared them for the apparitions of Mary. And each time Mary invited them to recite the Rosary. The devotion of the first Saturday for five consecutive months holds a special place in these messages.

During his pastoral visit to Portugal, Pope Benedict XVI said that in 1917, when the Virgin Mary appeared to the three simple shepherd children, "heaven opened like a window of hope above Portugal", and "This window of hope is opened by God when man closes the door to him."

Today, many have closed the door to God. If we, at the centenary of Fatima, want "heaven opened" to us and to others as "the window of hope" we must prepare well for it. We can do that by celebrating the Five First Saturdays and the consecration to the Immaculate Heart of Mary as found in the message of Fatima, which is the best way of venerating the Immaculate Heart of Mary. This booklet aims to be a source of support both now and later on, since we always need heaven as an open "window of hope".

In 2010 the Pope expressed a wish: "May the seven years which separate us from the centenary of the apparitions hasten the fulfilment of the prophecy of the triumph of the Immaculate Heart of Mary, to the glory of the Most Holy Trinity."[1] Thus he also announced the aim of the seven year preparation and the celebration of the centenary itself: the triumph of the Immaculate Heart of Mary. It is by celebrating the first Saturday of five consecutive months which significantly contributes to this triumph and will prepare us well for our commitment to the Immaculate Heart of Mary and, through this commitment, to the consecration to the Sacred Heart of Jesus and to the fruitful celebration of the centenary of the events in Fatima.

In short, our aim and the aim of heaven is the triumph of the Immaculate Heart of Mary. The way to this goal is, according to the desire of Jesus and Mary - as announced in the apparition of 13th July 1917, celebrating the devotion of the first Saturday of five consecutive months according to the message of Fatima, consecrating ourselves to her Heart, and living out this consecration.

For those who might be put off by this notion of the "triumph of the Immaculate Heart of Mary" as appearing to suggest she is taking precedence over God, it might be appropriate to explain the centuries-old understanding in the Church, especially by St Louis de Montfort, that Mary exists only to fulfil the holy will of God and lead souls to Jesus, and hence that this triumph of her Heart is God's will as the means to introduce the reign of the Sacred Heart of Jesus.[2]

The Immaculate Heart of Mary

The triumph of the Immaculate Heart of Mary is announced in the second part of the Fatima secret Mary shared with the shepherds on 13th July 1917. In this part, the heavenly Lady begins by saying that God wants to introduce the devotion to her Immaculate Heart to the world "to save souls". Then she conditionally foretells World War II, the horrors of Communism and the persecution of the Church. But this would not happen if people stopped offending God, celebrated the devotion of the first Saturday for five consecutive months, and if Russia was consecrated to the Immaculate Heart of Mary. In the final positive part, the ultimate triumph of the Immaculate Heart of Mary is announced: the consecration and conversion of Russia and world peace lasting for some time. The triumph of the Immaculate Heart of Mary is announced with the following words:

> The good will be martyred; the Holy Father will have much to suffer; various nations[3] will be annihilated. In the end, my Immaculate Heart will triumph. The Holy Father will consecrate Russia to me, and she shall be converted, and a period of peace will be granted to the world.

Lúcia Santos, Francisco and Jacinta Marto, 1917.

Mary's announcement has a double meaning. First, according to the seer Lucia, these words announce victory over the wars which prevent world peace. Let us have a look at Lucia's explanation in her last writing: *How I See the Message, in the Course of Time and in the Light of Events* which connects the triumph of the Immaculate Heart of Mary to the conversion of Russia and a period of peace:

> "In the end" - that is, after all this has happened - "my Immaculate Heart will triumph" over all the wars provoked throughout the world on account of the errors spread abroad by Russia "and a period of peace will be granted to the world". This promise refers to the wars provoked throughout the world by atheistic Communism, and it is over these wars that the Lady said her Immaculate Heart would triumph; it is to this that she is referring.[4]

When it comes to the Fatima messages, Lucia always stresses she only received them and that the Church has the right to interpret them.

> "I can state categorically that in the book Sister Lucia always displays great sureness and conviction when reproducing the message of Fatima, transcribing words from heaven that were given to her directly in the apparitions...She takes great care to avoid value judgements or interpretations, leaving the last word, and

submitting herself unconditionally, to the decision of the ecclesial Magisterium." (Serafim de Sousa Ferreira e Silva, Bishop of Fatima)[5]

The triumph of the Immaculate Heart of Mary and a life of faith

The second, deeper triumph of the Immaculate Heart of Mary, is a triumph in the heart of man and in communities acting according to the will of God. It was this deeper meaning Pope Benedict XVI meant when he visited Fatima in 2010 and said: "May the seven years which separate us from the centenary of the apparitions hasten the fulfilment of the prophecy of the triumph of the Immaculate Heart of Mary, to the glory of the Most Holy Trinity."[6]

On 26th June 2000, while then Cardinal Ratzinger and the Prefect of the Congregation for the Doctrine of the Faith, he commented on the third part of the Fatima secret. Along with other words he said: "To save souls" has emerged as the key word of the first and second parts of the "secret", and the key word of this third part is the threefold cry: "Penance, Penance, Penance!"...Then at the end of his letter, he mentioned another key expression of the "secret" which has become justly famous: "my Immaculate Heart will triumph". What does this mean? The Heart open to God, purified by contemplation of God, is stronger than guns and weapons of every kind.[7]

Later on, as Pope Benedict XVI, in the preface to the book *The Last Fatima Seer*, he wrote: "I was impressed by the comforting promise of the Virgin Most Holy, as a synthesis and precious seal to it: 'My Immaculate Heart will triumph'".[8]

The triumph of the Immaculate Heart of Mary is surely above all the triumph of the Sacred Heart of Jesus. Mary retains nothing for herself, but she gives everything to Christ who, with this triumph, wants to praise his Mother. Pope St John Paul II said: "if victory comes it will be brought by Mary. Christ will conquer through her, because he wants the Church's victories now and in the future to be linked to her."[9]

We too are called to co-operate with our spiritual Mother in preparing victories for her Immaculate Heart. What a wonderful task! The triumph of Mary will also be ours; it will be revealed in the noblest way when we are united with God in heaven. One form of co-operating with our Mother Mary is to celebrate the first Saturday of five consecutive months that was revealed in the message of Fatima.

Devotion of the Five First Saturdays

The oldest Fatima seer, Lucia dos Santos, was a postulant with the Dorothean Sisters in the Spanish town Pontevedra preparing to enter religious life. On 10th December 1925, she saw Mary with the child Jesus by her side, elevated on a luminous cloud in her cell. Mary asked her to spread the devotion of the first Saturday of five consecutive months, and promised the grace of salvation to those who will practise it. That is the great promise of the Immaculate Heart of Mary.[10]

The great promise was already announced to Lucia on 13th July 1917, in the second part of the Fatima secret. Mary also said: "To prevent this" - namely, World War II, famine and persecutions of the Church and the Holy Father - "I will come to ask for the consecration of Russia to my Immaculate Heart and the Communion of Reparation on the first Saturdays".[11]

This text reveals that celebrating first Saturdays (together with the consecration of Russia) is not just a means of salvation, but also a way to world peace and spiritual well being.

Let us have a close look at how Lucia received the great promise in 1925. On 17th December 1927, at the request of her spiritual director, Fr P Aparicio, SJ, she wrote a record in the third person of the vision in Pontevedra and the great promise of salvation:

> On 13th June 1917, the seer asked Mary "to take them to heaven". The most Holy Virgin answered:
>
> "Yes. I will take Jacinta and Francisco soon. But you are to stay here some time longer. Jesus wishes to make use of you to make me known and loved. He wants to establish in the world devotion to my Immaculate Heart. I promise salvation to those who embrace it, and those souls will be loved by God like flowers placed by me to adorn his throne."
>
> "Am I to stay here alone?" I asked sadly.
>
> "No, my daughter. Are you suffering a great deal? Don't lose heart. I will never forsake you. My Immaculate Heart will be your refuge and the way that will lead you to God".[12]
>
> On 10th December 1925, the most Holy Virgin appeared to her, and by her side, elevated on a luminous cloud, was a child. The most Holy Virgin rested her hand on her shoulder, and as she did so, she showed her a heart encircled by thorns, which she was holding in her other hand. At the same time, the child said:
>
> "Have compassion on the Heart of your Most Holy Mother, covered with thorns with which ungrateful men pierce at every moment, and there is no one to make an act of reparation to remove them."

Then the most Holy Virgin said:

"Look, my daughter, at my Heart, surrounded with thorns with which ungrateful men pierce every moment by their blasphemies and ingratitude. You at least try to console me and say that I promise to assist at the moment of death, with the graces necessary for salvation, all those who, on the first Saturday of five consecutive months shall confess, receive Holy Communion, recite five decades of the Rosary, and keep me company for fifteen minutes while meditating on the fifteen mysteries of the Rosary, with the intention of making reparation to me."[13]

It is necessary to distinguish between the devotion of the first Saturday and the devotion of the first Saturday of five consecutive months. The great promise of Mary to assist at the moment of death, with all the graces necessary for salvation refers to those who at least once in their life on the first Saturday of five consecutive months fulfil all five listed conditions. Pope Pius X already recommended the first Saturdays devotion before Fatima, where the intention is to fulfil all the conditions in reparation to the Immaculate Heart of Mary. The first Saturdays devotion had already been an established custom in the Catholic Church. On 1st July 1905, Pope Pius X approved and granted indulgences for the practice of the first Saturdays of twelve consecutive months in honour of the Immaculate Conception. This practice greatly resembled the reported request of Mary at the Pontevedra apparition. In addition, it is commendable to spend each first Saturday in the spirit of reparation and in prayer for vocations and the holiness of priests. According to the Fatima revelation the most complete form of the first Saturdays devotion consists in fulfilling all five conditions, which we will return to.

Jesus's commission

Celebrating Five First Saturdays is not only Mary's will, but also Jesus's will. He sent Mary in advance, and then he too strove to spread this devotion. In the previous chapter we saw that celebrating Five First Saturdays was Mary's will. When spreading this devotion, Lucia immediately ran into significant difficulties, and to fulfil her task, Jesus encouraged her to show that celebrating Five First Saturdays is not only Mary's will, but also his will. Let's take a look at Lucia's record of Jesus's intervention, as it was written in the letter to Fr Aparicio. On 15th February 1926, Lucia was about to empty the rubbish bin outside the garden. There she met a boy who asked her:

"Have you spread throughout the world what our heavenly Mother requested of you?"

With that, he was transformed into a resplendent child. Knowing then that it was Jesus, I said:

"My Jesus! You know very well what my confessor said to me in the letter I read to you. He told me that it was necessary for this vision to be repeated, for further happenings to prove its credibility, and he added that Mother Superior, on her own, could do nothing to propagate this devotion."

"It is true your Superior, alone, can do nothing, but with my grace, she can do all. It is enough that your confessor gives you permission, and that your Superior speak of it for it to be believed even without people knowing to whom it has been revealed."

"But my confessor said in his letter that this devotion is not lacking in the world, because there are many souls who receive you on the first Saturday of the month, in honour of Our Lady and the fifteen mysteries of the Rosary."

"It is true, my daughter, that many souls begin the first Saturdays, but few finish them, and those who do complete them do so in order to receive the graces that are promised thereby. It would please me more if they did five with fervour and with the intention of making reparation to the Heart of your heavenly Mother, than if they did fifteen, in a tepid and indifferent manner."[14]

In a revelation in March 1939, our Lord said to me once more:

"Ask, ask again insistently for the promulgation of the Communion of Reparation in honour of the Immaculate Heart of Mary on the first Saturdays. The time is coming

> when the rigour of my justice will punish the crimes of diverse nations. Some of them will be annihilated. At last the severity of my justice will fall severely on those who want to destroy my reign in souls."[15]

When the text speaks about punishments, we should know they are announced conditionally. It was Mary's intention to show humanity the way by which it could be saved from transient and eternal punishments (see the prophecy on 13th July): "If what I say to you is done, many souls will be saved and there will be peace, but if people do not cease offending God a worse war will break out…if my requests are heeded, Russia will be converted and there will be peace". She mentioned three main conditions for the world to be saved from war and other punishments: first, the conversion of humanity through the fulfilment of her request, second, the consecration of Russia and third, the Communion of Reparation on the first Saturdays.

Lucia's attempts to spread the devotion

Sister Lucia tried her best with her spiritual leaders and her bishop of Leiria - at the time it was José Correia da Silva - to introduce the devotion of the Five First Saturdays of five consecutive months.

The Bishop of Leiria confirmed the apparitions of Mary to the three shepherd children in the years 1916 and 1917 as authentic in his pastoral letter of 13th October 1930. And now Sister Lucia tried even harder to convince him that he should confirm and also request the spread of the devotion of the first Saturday of five consecutive months. On 28th October 1934, she wrote from the town of Pontevedra in Spain to Father Gonçalves:

"His Excellency the Bishop of Leiria has promised me he will start spreading the reparatory devotion to the Immaculate Heart of Mary next year; I hope the good God may also count on your co-operation."[16]

The seer of Fatima was aware that prevention of World War II and the persecutions of Christians depended also on the timely spreading of the first Saturdays devotion. She so ardently strove to convince him that she was considered "annoying".

On 19th March 1939, she wrote in her letter to Father Aparicio regarding the first five Saturdays devotion:

> War and peace in the world depend on the celebration of this devotion and the consecration to the Hearts of Jesus and Mary connected to it. Therefore I wished so much these were spread, and much more because it is the will of our good God and our beloved heavenly Mother.[17]

Despite Sister Lucia's persistent efforts, the devotion of the first Saturday of five consecutive months was not announced by the Bishop of Leiria until 13th September 1939, after World War II had begun on 1st September 1939.

He also had holy cards of Our Lady with the explanation of the devotion prepared. The devotion of the first Saturday of five consecutive months started to spread among people in dioceses and parishes not only in Portugal, but also elsewhere. The room of the apparitions was later turned into a chapel.

The Fatima seer was aware of the fact that this devotion should be spread all over the world. Therefore, on 2nd December 1940, she wrote to Pope Pius XII, asking him: "I ask your Holiness to spread this devotion all over the world." The devotion of the first Saturday of five consecutive months was accepted in many places in the world, however it did not last everywhere. Now it is being introduced again. The situation we live in today clearly shows that reconciliation and reparatory devotion is so much more necessary at this moment than in 1917 or 1925 when Sister Lucia received the message about it.

When the Holy Father John Paul II, on 25th March 1984, consecrated Russia and the whole world to the Immaculate Heart of Mary, this act brought about the fall of communist rule in the Soviet Union and other eastern countries, and the demolition of the Berlin Wall. We hope that the general introduction of the first Saturdays devotion connected to Christian life will lead to reinforcement of the faith among people, to peace and to the foretold total triumph of the Immaculate Heart of Mary.

To sum up the thoughts of Jesus, Mary and Lucia regarding celebrating the first Saturdays devotion we can say that by this devotion we comply with the desire of Jesus and Mary. We bring consolation to both of them and honour the Immaculate Heart of Mary in an excellent way and make reparation to it. It leads us to a warm childlike relationship with our heavenly Mother and promises us eternal salvation. In this way it gives or imparts a Marian character to our faith as it fully takes into account the mediatory role of Mary. At the same time it is a means of preventing wars and thus for the achievement of world peace. All these fruits, however, depend on our personal co-operation.

How to celebrate the Five First Saturdays devotion

In 1925 in Pontevedra, Spain, Mary promised she would assist us at the hour of death with the graces necessary for salvation if we, on the first Saturday of five consecutive months, fulfil the following five conditions:

1. Make a good confession in the spirit of reparation to the Immaculate Heart of Mary. We can go to Confession several days before or after the first Saturday, but we have to receive Holy Communion on the first Saturday in a state of sanctifying grace;

2. Receive Holy Communion: the central act in making the first Saturdays. Whoever cannot go to church,

e.g. the sick, can go to Confession and receive Holy Communion where they live;

3. Recite five decades of the Rosary;

4. Keep Mary company for fifteen minutes while meditating on one or more mysteries of the Rosary. We can pray and meditate at home;

5. Fulfil all four conditions mentioned with the intention to make reparation to the Immaculate Heart of Mary.

Jesus explained to Lucia that those who could not fulfil the conditions mentioned on Saturday, could with a priest's (e.g. confessor's) permission fulfil them for a justifiable reason the following Sunday. That permission would be of benefit and relief to many.

Whoever loves Jesus and Mary and his neighbours and also himself, will not attend or participate in the first Saturdays devotion only on the Five First Saturdays, but it may become a rule of life for him and an opportunity to prove his love of Jesus, the Virgin Mary and of all people. Our goal is following Christ as the Gospel teaches us. The Virgin Mary helps us to do this by celebrating the first Saturdays.

Those who are able to do that will celebrate the first Saturdays devotion in church together with others. A priest will be available for Confession. It is best to recite the Rosary with meditation before Holy Mass. After

Mass there is a litany of the blessed Virgin Mary in front of the Blessed Sacrament, renewal of dedication to the Immaculate Heart of Mary and Benediction. A priest will be available to the sick and the aged for Confession and Holy Communion where they live, but they will meditate on one or more mysteries and recite the Rosary themselves.

How Sister Lucia loved this devotion

Sister Lucia fervently mentioned this devotion again and again, which is revealed also in her letters. On 1st November 1927, she wrote to her Confirmation sponsor Maria Filomena de Miranda:

> I do not know whether you are already familiar with the reparatory devotion of the first Saturday of five consecutive months to the Immaculate Heart of Mary. As it is new I would like to advise you to make it as our dear heavenly Mother has asked for it, and Jesus revealed his wish to celebrate it. Moreover, it seems to me, my dear sponsor, it would be good you do not just get to know it and present consolation to Jesus by celebrating it, but that you also spread it and encourage also many other people to practise it…I am sure, my dear sponsor, that we can be happy to be able to give this proof of love to our dear heavenly Mother as we are blessed to know she wishes we offer it to her. As far as I am concerned, I never feel so happy as when the first

Saturday is drawing near. Is it not true that our greatest happiness is in belonging fully to Jesus and Mary and to love them, only and solely them, without reservations? We can see that very clearly in the lives of Saints... They were happy because they loved, my dear sponsor, and we must strive to love as they loved, but not only to have Jesus, that is less important - for if we did not have him on this earth, we would have him in heaven - but because of presenting Jesus and Mary with consolation to be loved...and that they in exchange for this love of ours can save many souls.[18]

The fact of a happy or an unhappy eternal life - our goal is heaven

If we take the devotion seriously, the Virgin Mary assures us not only temporary happiness (especially because of the absence of war) but also a happy eternal life in heaven. Today many do not believe in life after death or their faith is threatened by doubt. Are we ourselves firmly convinced that death is not the end, but that life is only the beginning? God reigns, eternity exists. Our souls are immortal! Jesus and Mary are waiting to see us alive and glorified in heaven. Our faith teaches us that. God affirms this again and again, also in an extraordinary way through apparitions of angels, the Virgin Mary and also Jesus himself.

That happened in Fatima, Portugal, when the Angel of Peace and the Virgin Mary appeared to the three children and addressed them. The events in Fatima are, like every authentic apparition, first proof for the existence of the living God, the Virgin Mary, angels and Saints. The three Fatima shepherds, a nine year-old Lucia, an eight year-old Francisco, and a six year-old Jacinta experienced an encounter with the world of God in a threefold meeting with the angel in 1916, and also the next year when the Virgin Mary appeared to them six times and addressed them.

The heavenly Mother told the little shepherds already during the first apparition on 13th May 1917, that she was from heaven, and she also assured them they would be there themselves one day. For Lucia took courage and asked her:

"And will I go to heaven, too?"
"Yes, you will."
"And Jacinta?"
"She will go also."
"And Francisco?"
"He will go there too, but he must say many Rosaries."

Also Mary's answer to Lucia's question whether two of her deceased friends are already in heaven speaks of the fact of life after death. Mary said for the first one she is already saved, but that the other is still in Purgatory.

At Mary's assurance she would go to heaven, Lucia said: "The inner joy I felt then was indescribable." St Paul expressed himself similarly when he said: "the things that no eye has seen and no ear has heard, things beyond the mind of man, all that God has prepared for those who love him." (1 *Co* 2:9)

A person can voluntarily exclude himself or herself from heaven

According to the teachings of Scripture God does not wish "that any should perish but that all should reach repentance." (2 *Pt* 3:9) God "wants everyone to be saved and reach full knowledge of the truth" (1 *Tm* 2:4) but it depends on the free will of people whether they will reach that goal or not. The *Compendium of the Catechism of the Catholic Church* teaches that God "has created the human person to be free and responsible; and he respects our decisions. Therefore, it is the human person who freely excludes himself from communion with God if at the moment of death he persists in mortal sin and refuses the merciful love of God." (213)

The Virgin Mary, who is our spiritual Mother, wants to help us and encourages us to live a responsible life. Therefore for love of us and with God's consent she showed the children in Fatima for a brief moment the horror of hell. In that horrible moment they saw how the souls of poor sinners suffer in hell like in a sea of fire.

The expression of Mary's merciful love for us sinners is her request that after each decade of the Rosary we should say:

O my Jesus, forgive us our sins,
save us from the fires of hell,
lead all souls to heaven,
especially those
who have most need of your mercy.

The truth of the existence of hell is based on Holy Scripture. When Jesus in Matthew's Gospel speaks on the last judgement, he says to those on his left the following words:

> Go away from me, with your curse upon you, to the eternal fire prepared for the devil and his angels. For I was hungry and you never gave me food; I was thirsty and you never gave me anything to drink; I was a stranger and you never made me welcome, naked and you never clothed me, sick and in prison and you never visited me. (*Mt* 25:41-43)

With these words Jesus does not want to frighten us, but to direct us to good deeds and to a longing for heaven.

Whoever doubts the existence of eternal life should ask himself: "And what if it is true that God exists, that heaven and hell exist? What is safer: faith or unbelief? Have I tried hard enough to get to know the truth? I live only once! I must not play with eternity! And what if it is true that Jesus died on the cross for love of me to gain eternal happiness with him in heaven, and I do not care for him? And even his love does not move me? What can convince me, then, if his love does not move me?"

We save people for heaven by prayer and sacrifice

On 13th May 1917, in Fatima Mary told Francisco he had to say many Rosaries before he went to heaven. This stipulation holds good for all of us. St Alfonsus Maria Liguori was correct in saying: "Only the one can live right who can pray right. Whoever prays will be saved; whoever does not pray will be condemned."

Mary wants to remind us of the necessity of prayer. With prayer we grow in faith, hope and love and unite ourselves to God, who is our ultimate goal and the meaning of our entire life.

Already during his first apparition in the spring of 1916, the Angel of Peace taught the Fatima shepherds a special prayer which is also quite appropriate as a preparation for the centenary of Fatima:

My God! I believe,
I adore, I hope,
and I love you.
I ask pardon of you for those
who do not believe, do not adore,
do not hope, and do not love you.

The three theological virtues, faith, hope and charity, and prayer are the basis and the alphabet of every Christian life. We already received these virtues at holy Baptism as the foundation that must be developed throughout our lives by the help of God's grace. They are like flowers we have to water steadily and by the help of the Holy Spirit live them out.

We not only awaken faith, hope and charity, but we also ask forgiveness for those who live without faith, hope and charity. In this way we join Jesus on the cross, who did not judge or even curse his enemies, but asked his Father: "Father, forgive them; they do not know what they are doing." (*Lk* 23:34)

In this light, Fatima is a call to a deeper faith, hope and charity. In the words of St John Paul II, it is more urgent today than ever. At the same time it is an invitation to praise God, to make reparation for those who do not believe in God, do not adore him, do not hope in him and do not love him. From the beginning the shepherd children were invited by the angel to engage in apostolic work, to save people for heaven, first of all by praying for them. In this way they themselves grew in love not only for God, but also for their neighbour.

Prayer together with sacrifice offered to God for love of him and neighbour is particularly redemptive. The little shepherds of Fatima were strongly encouraged to save people for heaven by repeated requests of Mary, and especially by the vision of hell. They prayed and sacrificed themselves very much for this purpose. No sacrifice was too difficult for them. By doing this they made themselves holy. For this Francisco and Jacinta were beatified in 2000 by St John Paul II and with the permission of the Holy See the diocesan cause for the beatification for Lucia began in 2008.

May their heroic example encourage us to save people for heaven by prayer and sacrifice. Sacrifice accepted for love of God and neighbour and united to Christ on the cross gains value from his sacrifice. Therefore it is the most effective prayer and more than prayer. It is not necessary to seek opportunities for sacrifice since every day brings something difficult where our patience is tried. Many times already the duties of our profession and state are connected with the cross.

In eternity we will realise how many people were saved by God for heaven on the basis of our prayers and sacrifices. Therefore we will gladly listen to Mary who on 19th August 1917, with a sad expression told them: "Pray, pray very much, and make sacrifices for sinners, for many souls go to hell because there are none to sacrifice themselves and to pray for them."

Jesus wants devotion to the Immaculate Heart of Mary

When we mention the Hearts of Jesus and Mary, we think of their person with all their inner richness, above all with their love. Here the heart is a symbol that indicates the profound spiritual reality.

To venerate the Immaculate Heart of Mary means to admire, devote ourselves to Mary and meditate on her spiritual life with all the virtues, above all with her love for

God and neighbour. In this devotion she shapes our heart after the Sacred Heart of Jesus.

First Saturdays are just one form of devotion to the Immaculate Heart of Mary. We will understand them better if we connect them with the events in Fatima. It is the Heart of Mary that takes the central place in the message of Fatima. In the second apparition to the three little shepherds on 13th June 1917, Mary said she would soon take Jacinta and Francisco to heaven. But to Lucia, she announced:

> But you are to stay here some time longer. Jesus wishes to make use of you to make me known and loved. He wants to establish in the world devotion to my Immaculate Heart. I promise salvation to those who embrace it, and those souls will be loved by God as flowers placed by me to adorn his throne.

Lucia received here her life's mission: to spread the devotion to the Immaculate Heart of Mary. To fulfil that wonderful mission as well as she could, God granted her almost a hundred years of a spiritually rich and an apostolically active life. Before Jacinta's early death, she also encouraged Lucia to spread devotion to the Immaculate Heart of Mary:

> It will not be long now before I go to heaven. You will remain here to make known that God wishes to

establish in the world devotion to the Immaculate Heart of Mary. When you are to say this, don't go and hide. Tell everybody that God grants us graces through the Immaculate Heart of Mary; that people are to ask her for them; and that the Heart of Jesus wants the Immaculate Heart of Mary to be venerated at his side. Tell them also to pray to the Immaculate Heart of Mary for peace since God has entrusted it to her.

Sense of reparation and the Immaculate Heart of Mary

Humankind with its sins has turned away from God and runs the risk of eternal damnation. Mary, as Mother of the human race, is concerned about our eternal destiny; therefore she, by her apparitions in Fatima, warns us that in turning our eyes too much to the cares of this world, we have forgotten the Last Things. She wants to help us to the right understanding and love. So she revealed her Immaculate Heart to us to save us and lead us to the depths of the Heart of Jesus.

After the second apparition, on 13th June 1917, the little shepherds saw in the right hand of Mary a heart surrounded by thorns. It seemed to Lucia that they pierced it. The little shepherds understood the Immaculate Heart of Mary had been offended by sins of humankind and was seeking reparation. From the time of that apparition they felt a more ardent love for the Immaculate Heart of Mary in their hearts. In this way, they grew spiritually, for love is the power that alone can change and sanctify a person. The heart they saw was a sign of love and a symbol of Mary's entire inner wealth whereby they too grew spiritually rich.

The first Saturdays devotion is above all directed to make reparation for ingratitude to the Immaculate Heart of Mary.

The word *reparation* in the messages of Fatima is not immediately evident to us. There is a connection between *reparation* and *reconciliation*. We say that we shall make reparation for our sins and the sins of others. Thus we want to emphasise our contribution that is necessary for God's forgiveness of sins and their consequences. Neither Mary nor Jesus need our reparation for themselves - but they ask for it, in the first Saturdays devotion - although they are hurt by our sins, which is shown also by the thorns around the heart in Mary's hand. It is us, people on earth, who need reparation and reconciliation when our relationships with Jesus and Mary are broken or shaken, to be re-established, or strengthened again so our souls can heal. The *Catechism of the Catholic Church* teaches us: "But sin also injures and weakens the sinner himself, as well as his relationships with God and neighbour." (1459). Our union with Jesus and Mary, and naturally with our neighbour, has to return to normality and begin to live in love again.

Jesus on the cross made reparation for all our sins and reconciled us with the Father, but we too have to co-operate with the requirement for conversion and reconciliation in order to gain fullness of spiritual health and model ourselves on Christ. By reparation and reconciliation we, with God's help, repair various disorders caused by sin. At the same time we show our co-operation and prepare ourselves to accept God's gifts. In our hearts the Holy Spirit is acting; we are shaping ourselves after the Hearts of Mary and Jesus. "The One who created you without yourself, won't save you without yourself," said St Augustine.

Devotion to the Immaculate Heart of Mary leads us to heaven

Pope Benedict XVI, as a pilgrim to the shrine of Fatima in 2010, said: "In Fatima, the Virgin Mary invites us all to look at the earth as the place of our pilgrimage towards the final homeland, which is heaven. Indeed we all are pilgrims and need a mother to lead us."

Devotion to the Immaculate Heart of Mary is according to God's will a means to save people for eternal happiness; a means that leads to conversion and a holy life of faith, hope and love, and to the final triumph of the Immaculate Heart of Mary. Mary revealed the purpose for the devotion to her Immaculate Heart to the three children in Fatima on 13th July 1917, after the vision of hell in the second part of the Fatima secret. Lucia tells: "Terrified and as if to plead for succour, we looked up at Our Lady, who said to us, so kindly and so sadly: 'You have seen hell, where the souls of poor sinners go. To save them God wishes to establish in the world devotion to my Immaculate Heart.'"

The Immaculate Heart of Mary beats for us and wants to save us for a happy eternity. Holy heaven bows to sinful earth. In a time of fast growth in indifference about faith, the Virgin Mary calls to the whole world: "People awake! It matters how you live. Do not be buried in the earth alone! God is merciful and expects you to convert and start to live a new life!"

What Mary achieved with the three children, she would also like to achieve with us. The little shepherds always had heaven in front of them as their goal. With great sacrifices they were saving sinners for heaven. Do we want to imitate them at least a bit?

Consecration to the Immaculate Heart of Mary

Consecration (commitment) to the Immaculate Heart of Mary is the supreme form of devotion to the Mother of God as we, in a way, enter her Heart which becomes our home. If we also live according to the consecration, we contribute a great deal to the final triumph of the Immaculate Heart of Mary. The Virgin Mary will welcome us to the glory of heaven after our death. However we will secretly take part in the overture to this glory already on the earth. It is the Fatima message through which consecration to the Immaculate Heart of Mary has been spread all over the world.

Consecration to the Immaculate Heart of Mary is a complete and irrevocable offering of ourselves to our spiritual Mother, and through her, to Jesus Christ. We put ourselves not only into her hands, but also her possession so that we may live freely at her disposal. As a matter of fact, it is all about the renewal of our baptismal promises. In this way St John Paul II committed himself to our Mother Mary with his papal motto that had become his life's orientation: "Totus tuus!"

The heart of the consecration is a conscious and total renunciation of sin, the seduction of evil and the devil, and

Our Lady of Fatima.

an irrevocable offering to the Heart of Mary and through it, to the Heart of Jesus as a response to their love. By the consecration, we make a deliberate renewal of our baptismal consecration to God.

The better the consecration is prepared, the more fruitful it is. By no means is it enough to recite the consecration prayer only. It is also necessary to live in accordance with it. We have to think, speak and do as Mary and Jesus do. This commitment reaches deeply into our lives and leads us along the way to conversion and new life. That is a life that comes from Baptism and the other sacraments, a life according to the Gospel, faithfully following Christ and Mary.

If we live out of this consecration, the prophecy of Ezekiel will be fulfilled in us:

> I shall give you a new heart, and put a new spirit in you; I shall remove the heart of stone from your bodies and give you a heart of flesh instead. I shall put my spirit in you, and make you keep my laws and sincerely respect my observances. (*Ezk* 36:26-27)

Our consecration to Mary does not stop at Mary, but through her it is directed to God. Mary is closest to God. If we commit ourselves to her, we will reach God in the fastest and most certain way. It is best if, in the text of dedication to Mary, we also express our consecration to Jesus. Through Mary to Jesus! We dedicate ourselves to Mary totally in order to be totally consecrated to Jesus and thus to the Father. As the Virgin Mary is full of the Holy Spirit he acts in us and sanctifies us better through our dedication to Mary.

Different forms of consecration

The highest form of consecration (commitment) to the Immaculate Heart of Mary is the consecration of the entire Church and the world. It was performed by Pope Pius XII on 31st October 1942. Beside the consecration of individuals, Portugal's bishops also carried it out in 1938. The Pope renewed it in the presence of the cardinals in the most solemn way in the basilica of St Peter on 8th December 1942. Since then, the Church and the world have been entrusted and dedicated to the Immaculate Heart of Mary just as they were consecrated to the Sacred Heart of Jesus in 1899 by Pope Leo XIII.

On 25th March 1984, Pope John Paul II, in union with all the bishops in the world, consecrated the Church and the whole world to the Immaculate Heart of Mary at St Peter's Square after a solemn Mass. He added the words referring to the Russian people: "Especially enlighten the people whose consecration and commitment you expect from us." In this way he fulfilled God's wish that the Virgin Mary passed to Lucia on 13th June 1929 in the town of Tuy, Spain, in the Sisters' convent: "The moment has come in which God asks the Holy Father, in union with all the bishops of the world, to make the consecration of Russia to my Immaculate Heart, promising to save it by this means."

After this extremely important act of consecration, the collapse of Communism began that led to the downfall of the Soviet Union and other communist regimes and to the demolition of the Berlin Wall.

In the Jubilee Year of 2000, Pope John Paul II renewed that consecration and invited the bishops of all the world to Rome. Then on Sunday 8th October, together with more than fifteen hundred bishops, representatives of the universal episcopate, in front of Our Lady's statue, he made the act of consecration to our Mother Mary, Dawn of Salvation.

In the Year of Priests on 12th May 2010, Pope Benedict XVI consecrated all priests to the Immaculate Heart of Mary while he was in Fatima, and on Saturday 12th October 2013 Pope Francis consecrated all Marian movements and associations.

Apart from the consecration of humankind and the Church, God is also pleased with the consecrations of nations, dioceses, parishes, professions, families and individuals. On 13th May 1931, the Portuguese bishops became the first in history to consecrate their country to the Immaculate Heart of Mary. Dioceses and parishes in Portugal also decided to consecrate themselves to the Immaculate Heart and renew the consecration. By it, Portuguese bishops spared their homeland from World War II and Communism.

In April 1943 Pope Pius XII asked all the bishops in the world to venerate the Immaculate Heart of Mary and to consecrate their dioceses to it in a special way. Many bishops responded to his invitation and consecrated their dioceses and/or their people to the Immaculate Heart of Mary.

Consecration and its regular renewal should lead us to a deeper Christian life. In this way, devotion to the Immaculate Heart of Mary will not be a mere "devotion", but will, in the example of Mary and with aid of her intercession, promote spiritual growth from the Word of God and the sacraments, especially from the Eucharist. It will have a positive influence on the new evangelisation.

If we practise devotion to the Immaculate Heart of Mary, commit ourselves to it, celebrate the first Saturdays and strive to live according to the will of God, what Mary promised to a ten year-old Lucia at the second apparition on 13th June 1917 will hold true for us: "Don't lose heart. I will never forsake you. My Immaculate Heart will be your refuge and the way that will lead you to God."

Mary will also intercede for us and will shape our hearts after her own. In this way we will like her, treasure the words of God in our hearts and meditate on them (cf. *Lk* 2:19; 51).

I am the Lady of the Rosary

Reciting the Rosary is very much emphasised with the devotion of the first Saturday and is an excellent and proven way that leads to the triumph of the Immaculate Heart of Mary. We not only pray one part of the Rosary, but we also meditate on one or more of the mysteries for fifteen minutes. So we dedicate a bit more than half an hour to the Rosary.

Reciting the Rosary has been recommended by popes in recent centuries, but also by Mary in several apparitions recognised by the Church, especially in Lourdes and Fatima. This precious prayer is very much in the forefront of the apparitions in Fatima. Mary always held the beads in her hands during those apparitions. She always asked the shepherd children to recite the Rosary every day. They prayed it even though their families did not use to say it together regularly. The little shepherds also recited it before the beginning of apparitions.

After the first apparition of Mary when Lucia and Jacinta told Francisco he would go to heaven, but at the request of Mary, he would have to say many Rosaries, he exclaimed very satisfied: "Oh my dear Lady! I will say as many Rosaries as you want!" He often moved away from

Lucia and Jacinta and recited or meditated the Rosary by himself. When Lucia tried to persuade him to play with them, he answered: "I will pray later as well. Don't you remember Our Lady said I should say many Rosaries?"

During the last apparition on 13th October 1917, Mary revealed that she was "the Lady of the Rosary." She told the shepherds: "Continue always to pray the Rosary every day!" Thus the Rosary became their lifelong prayer.

Reciting the Rosary bore abundant fruit. Once a mother and her son asked Francisco to obtain healing for the father and a grace for the son so that he would not need to join the army. Francisco invited them to kneel and recite the Rosary together. Other people joined them as well. On the way to the Cova da Iria they recited the second part of the Rosary together, and at the Cova da Iria the third one. Soon the mother and her son returned to the Cova da Iria together with the healed father.

Lucia tells of a man crying like a child who came to Jacinta. He had been called up by the army, but he had a sick wife in bed and three small children. He asked for either the healing of his wife or the call up to be withdrawn. Jacinta invited him to recite the Rosary with her. Then she said to him: "Do not cry! Mary is so good! Surely she will grant you the grace you are asking for."

Lucia did not forget the man. At the end of the Rosary she always said a Hail Mary for him. After a few months he came back with his wife and three small children to thank her for both graces he had received. Because of the fever he had caught, he was exempt from military service and his wife was miraculously healed by Mary.

Francisco and Jacinta held their rosaries in the hand especially in their last illness. Their mother said they recited from seven to eight Rosaries a day.

Sister Lucia on the Rosary

In her last booklet Sister Lucia wrote among other things the following on the Rosary:

> But, I ask myself: why were we to pray the Rosary? Why did she not choose some other prayer? …possibly because it was more accessible to everyone, little and great, wise and ignorant, so that, with good will, we can all, every day, offer to God the humble prayer of the five mysteries of the Rosary, which will enable us, from the very beginning, to plunge into and to live the principal mysteries of God and his redeeming work accomplished by Jesus Christ our Saviour.
>
> We begin this prayer by invoking the Holy Trinity: *In the name of the Father and of the Son and of the Holy Spirit*, after which we plunge into the first revelation which God gave us of this mystery: "The Holy Spirit will come upon you," the angel answered, "and the power of the Most High will cover you with its shadow. And so the child will be holy and will be called Son of God." (*Lk* 1:35)

And we continue our prayer gazing at Our Lady who is here transformed into a living temple of the most Blessed Trinity: the Holy Spirit which came down upon her, the Father who extended his work over her, and the Son whom the Most High generated in her virginal womb. This mystery of the most Blessed Trinity is the basis, the beginning and the end of all our prayer, of all our being and of the whole of our lives; we came from God, we are going to God and in God we live.

We very much need Our Lady to intercede for us before God. St John Paul II was right when he said that the prayer of the Rosary is his "favourite prayer". It is indeed the most beautiful prayer taught to us by heaven, and one which raises us to a deeper knowledge of God and of his redeeming work in Christ.[19]

Basilica of Our Lady of the Rosary, Sanctuary of Fatima, Portugal.

Triumph of the Immaculate Heart of Mary

At the beginning we set ourselves a task to co-operate with the preparation of the triumph of the Immaculate Heart of Mary. Reading this booklet we realise what fruits an active co-operation with the Five First Saturdays according to the Fatima apparitions brings to us. At the same time it is an excellent preparation for commitment and consecration to the Immaculate Heart of Mary and through it to the Sacred Heart of Jesus. In this way we will actively co-operate with the preparation for the triumph of the Immaculate Heart of Mary.

The triumph of the Immaculate Heart of Mary will first start in our hearts when we allow our Mother Mary to shape our hearts after the Sacred Heart of Jesus. When we strive for faithfulness in following Christ, our lives will bear fruit. And after death we will come to him and to our Mother in heaven.

The Immaculate Heart of Mary will triumph also in our communities, in our families, parishes and dioceses and in the entire Church and, as Jesus foretold, the gates of hell shall not prevail against it. (cf. *Mt* 16:18) His words hold true: "In the world you will have trouble, but be brave: I have conquered the world." (*Jn* 16:33) For he has promised:

"I am with you always; yes, to the end of time." (*Mt* 28:20) He is with us if we are gathered in his name, in his love and unity. For he assured us what holds true for common prayer, but also for our life: "For where two or three meet in my name, I shall be there with them." (*Mt* 18:20)

And what will we do?

- We will celebrate the first Saturday of five consecutive months in the Fatima way in the parish or community, or individually.

- After the fifth first Saturday we will on the same day or on some other appropriate day commit and consecrate ourselves to the Immaculate Heart of Mary and through it to the Sacred Heart of Jesus.

- We can consecrate ourselves as individuals, as a family or a parish, a diocese or the Church in an individual country in agreement with the appropriate Church leadership. In this respect a suitable formula should be chosen. There are some formulas at the end of the booklet, or suitable formulas common in local churches.

- To preserve the initial zeal it is necessary often, at least once a year, to renew the consecration after a good preparation.

- For preparation of consecration to live out consecration some prayer formulas are available.

The person who consecrates himself or herself, tries his or her best to:

1. Live a consistent life according to the Gospel;
2. Sanctify Sundays and obligatory feasts;
3. Pray regularly and recite the Rosary;
4. Observe the devotion of first Fridays and first Saturdays;
5. Foster mutual love in the family and help people in spiritual and physical need;
6. Renew and spread the consecration.

Texts to Accompany the Rosary

To recite the Rosary more easily in accordance with the message of Fatima, Bible texts can be used. Slowly, thinking of the Virgin Mary with whom we keep company, we read the text before each decade, meditating on it in silence for a while. We can also meditate on one of the mysteries for fifteen minutes, perhaps at the end of the prayer, as Sister Lucia did.

Joyful Mysteries

The Annunciation

In the sixth month the angel Gabriel was sent by God to a town in Galilee called Nazareth, to a virgin betrothed to a man named Joseph, of the House of David; and the virgin's name was Mary. He went in and said to her, "Rejoice, so highly favoured! The Lord is with you." She was deeply disturbed by these words and asked herself what this greeting could mean, but the angel said to her, "Mary, do not be afraid; you have won God's favour. Listen! You are to conceive and bear a son, and you must name him Jesus . He will be great and will be called the Son of the Most High. The Lord God will give him the throne of his ancestor David; he will rule over the House of Jacob for ever and his reign will have no end." Mary said to the angel, "But how can this come about, since I am a virgin?" "The Holy Spirit will come upon you" the angel answered "and the power of the Most High will cover you with its shadow. And so the child will be holy and will be called Son of God. Know this too: your kinswoman Elizabeth has, in her old age, herself conceived a son, and she whom people called barren is now in her sixth month, for nothing is impossible to God." "I am the handmaid of the Lord," said Mary "let what you have said be done to me." And the angel left her. (*Lk* 1:26-38)

Oh Mary with your "Yes" you have opened heaven's ways. You have fulfilled the will of the Father. You will be blessed for ever: your intercession is heard in heaven because you have accepted God's plan. Let us pray that we can always say "Yes" to the Father. Mary, help us to be humble and obedient to God's will.

The Visitation

Mary set out at that time and went as quickly as she could to a town in the hill country of Judah. She went into Zechariah's house and greeted Elizabeth. Now as soon as Elizabeth heard Mary's greeting, the child leapt in her womb and Elizabeth was filled with the Holy Spirit. She gave a loud cry and said, "Of all women you are the most blessed, and blessed is the fruit of your womb. Why should I be honoured with a visit from the mother of my Lord? For the moment your greeting reached my ears, the child in my womb leapt for joy. Yes, blessed is she who believed that the promise made her by the Lord would be fulfilled."

And Mary said:

"My soul proclaims the greatness of the Lord / and my spirit exults in God my saviour; / because he has looked upon his lowly handmaid. / Yes, from this day forward all generations will call me blessed, / for the Almighty has done great things for me. / Holy is his name..." (*Lk* 1:39-49)

Mary goes to visit Elizabeth. She carries God to her cousin, for the love of her brothers and neighbours. Lord, help us to carry Christ to others like Mary did. Let us ask Mary for the gift of burning charity.

The Nativity

While they were there the time came for her to have her child, and she gave birth to a son, her first-born. She wrapped him in swaddling clothes, and laid him in a manger because there was no room for them at the inn. In the countryside close by there were shepherds who lived in the fields and took it in turns to watch their flocks during the night. The angel of the Lord appeared to them and the glory of the Lord shone round them. They were terrified, but the angel said, "Do not be

> afraid. Listen, I bring you news of great joy, a joy to be shared by the whole people. Today in the town of David a saviour has been born to you; he is Christ the Lord. And here is a sign for you: you will find a baby wrapped in swaddling clothes and lying in a manger." (*Lk* 2:6-12)

Infant Jesus in the manger, Mary, Joseph and the shepherds adore him. Let us also adore Christ, the Son of God, in the silence of our souls and from the depths of our hearts. Let us ask Mary to make us love Jesus more, and also for the gift of poverty of spirit.

The Presentation in the Temple

> And when the day came for them to be purified as laid down by the Law of Moses, they took him up to Jerusalem to present him to the Lord - observing what stands written in the Law of the Lord: Every first-born male must be consecrated to the Lord - and also to offer in sacrifice, in accordance with what is said in the Law of the Lord, a pair of turtledoves or two young pigeons. Now in Jerusalem there was a man named Simeon. He was an upright and devout man; he looked forward to Israel's comforting and the Holy Spirit rested on him. It had been revealed to him by the Holy Spirit that he would not see death until he had set eyes on the Christ of the Lord. Prompted by the Spirit he came to the Temple; and when the parents brought in the child Jesus to do for

> him what the Law required, he took him into his arms and blessed God; and he said:
>
> "Now, Master, you can let your servant go in peace, / just as you promised; / because my eyes have seen the salvation / which you have prepared for all the nations to see, / a light to enlighten the pagans / and the glory of your people Israel".
>
> As the child's father and mother stood there wondering at the things that were being said about him, Simeon blessed them and said to Mary his mother, "You see this child: he is destined for the fall and rising of many in Israel, destined to be a sign that is rejected - and a sword will pierce your own soul too - so that the secret thoughts of many may be laid bare". (*Lk* 2:22-35)

We need to pay attention to the voice of God, to discern his call and accept the mission he gave us. After Simeon's prophecy, Mary takes into her Heart the wound of sorrow, but in the silence she accepts the will of her Father.

The Finding of Jesus in the Temple

> Every year his parents used to go to Jerusalem for the feast of the Passover. When he was twelve years old, they went up for the feast as usual. When they were on their way home after the feast, the boy Jesus stayed behind in Jerusalem without his parents knowing it. They assumed he was with the caravan, and it was only

after a day's journey that they went to look for him among their relations and acquaintances. When they failed to find him they went back to Jerusalem looking for him everywhere. Three days later, they found him in the Temple, sitting among the doctors, listening to them, and asking them questions; and al those who heard him were astounded at his intelligence and his replies. They were overcome when they saw him, and his mother said to him, "My child, why have you done this to us? See how worried your father and I have been, looking for you." "Why were you looking for me?" he replied "Did you not know that I must be busy with my Father's affairs?" But they did not understand what he meant. He then went down with them and came to Nazareth and lived under their authority. His mother stored up all these things in her heart. (*Lk* 2:41-51)

Let us think of how many times we have been far from Jesus; from that Jesus, who with so much love has died for us. Let us meditate that in the difficulties of life the only safety is finding Jesus and never again leaving his great love.

Luminous mysteries

The Baptism of Jesus

Then Jesus appeared: he came from Galilee to the Jordan to be baptised by John. John tried to dissuade him. "It is I who need baptism from you" he said "and yet you come to me!" But Jesus replied, "Leave it like this for the time being; it is fitting that we should, in this way, do all that righteousness demands". At this, John gave in to him. As soon as Jesus was baptised he came up from the water, and suddenly the heavens opened and he saw the Spirit of God descending like a dove and coming down on him. And a voice spoke from heaven, "This is my Son, the Beloved; my favour rests on him". (*Mt* 3:13-17)

The Baptism in the Jordan is first of all a mystery of light. Here, as Christ descends into the waters, the innocent one who became "sin" for our sake (cf. 2 *Co* 5:21), the heavens open wide and the voice of the Father declares him the beloved Son (cf. *Mt* 3:17) while the Spirit descends on him to invest him with the mission which he is to carry out.

The Wedding Feast at Cana

Three days later there was a wedding at Cana in Galilee. The mother of Jesus was there, and Jesus and his disciples had also been invited. When they ran out of wine, since the wine provided for the wedding was all finished, the mother of Jesus said to him, "They have no wine". Jesus said, "Woman, why turn to me? My hour has not come yet. His mother said to the servants, "Do whatever he tells you". There were six stone water jars standing there, meant for the ablutions that are customary among

> the Jews: each could hold twenty or thirty gallons. Jesus said to the servants, "Fill the jars with water", and they filled them to the brim. "Draw some out now" he told them "and take it to the steward." They did this; the steward tasted the water, and it had turned into wine. Having no idea where it came from - only the servants who had drawn the water knew - the steward called the bridegroom and said, "People generally serve the best wine first, and keep the cheaper sort till the guests have had plenty to drink; but you have kept the best wine till now". This was the first of the signs given by Jesus: it was given at Cana in Galilee. He let his glory be seen, and his disciples believed in him. (*Jn* 2:1-12)

Another mystery of light is the first of the signs, given at Cana, when Christ changes water into wine and opens the hearts of the disciples to faith, thanks to the intervention of Mary, the first among believers.

The Proclamation of the Kingdom of God

> Jesus went into Galilee. There he proclaimed the Good News from God. "The time has come" he said "and the kingdom of God is close at hand. Repent, and believe the Good News."(*Mk* 1:14-15)

The preaching by which Jesus proclaims the coming of the Kingdom of God, calls to conversion and forgives the sins of all who draw near to him in humble trust (cf. *Mk* 2:3-

13; *Lk* 7:47-48): the inauguration of that ministry of mercy which he continues to exercise until the end of the world, particularly through the Sacrament of Reconciliation which he has entrusted to his Church (cf. *Jn* 20:22-23).

The Transfiguration

> Now about eight days after this had been said, he took with him Peter and John and James and went up the mountain to pray. As he prayed, the aspect of his face was changed and his clothing became brilliant as lightning. Suddenly there were two men there talking to him; they were Moses and Elijah appearing in glory, and they were speaking of his passing which he was to accomplish in Jerusalem. Peter and his companions were heavy with sleep, but they kept awake and saw his glory and the two men standing with him. As these were leaving him, Peter said to Jesus, "Master, it is wonderful for us to be here; so let us make three tents, one for you, one for Moses and one for Elijah". He did not know what he was saying. As he spoke, a cloud came and covered them with shadow; and when they went into the cloud the disciples were afraid. And a voice came from the cloud saying, "This is my Son the Chosen One. Listen to him." And after the voice had spoken, Jesus was found alone. The disciples kept silence and, at that time, told no one what they had seen. (*Lk* 9:28-36)

The mystery of light par excellence is the Transfiguration, traditionally believed to have taken place on Mount Tabor. The glory of the Godhead shines forth from the face of Christ as the Father commands the astonished apostles to "listen to him" (cf. *Lk* 9:35) and to prepare to experience with him the agony of the Passion, so as to come with him to the joy of the Resurrection and a life transfigured by the Holy Spirit.

The Institution of the Eucharist

> And as they were eating he took some bread, and when he had said the blessing he broke it and gave it to them. "Take it," he said "this is my body." Then he took a cup, and when he had returned thanks he gave it to them, and all drank from it, and he said to them, "This is my blood, the blood of the covenant, which is to be poured out for many. I tell you solemnly, I shall not drink any more wine until the day I drink the new wine in the kingdom of God." (*Mk* 14:22-25)

A final mystery of light is the institution of the Eucharist, in which Christ offers his body and blood as food under the signs of bread and wine, and testifies "to the end" his love for humanity (*Jn* 13:1) for whose salvation he will offer himself in sacrifice.

Sorrowful mysteries

The Agony of Jesus in the Garden

Then Jesus came with them to a small estate called Gethsemane; and he said to his disciples, “Stay here while I go over there to pray”. He took Peter and the two sons of Zebedee with him. And sadness came over him, and great distress. Then he said to them, “My soul is sorrowful to the point of death. Wait here and keep awake with me.” And going on a little further he fell on his face and prayed. “My Father,” he said, “if it is possible, let this cup pass me by. Nevertheless, let it be as you, not I, would have it.” (*Mt* 26:36-39)

In his anguish he prayed even more earnestly, and his sweat fell to the ground like great drops of blood. (*Lk* 22:44)

In the prayer of abandonment to the Father, Jesus found strength and trust, and an angel was sent to comfort him. So Jesus will be our comforting angel. It’s as he said to us: “Why do you worry about your difficulties? Be strong in me; look to your God in your most troubled hour, and you will be triumphant.” Let us ask to abandon ourselves in God and always do his will.

The Scourging of Jesus at Pillar

When morning came, all the chief priests and the elders of the people met in council to bring about the death of Jesus. They had him bound, and led him away to hand him over to Pilate, the governor. When he found that Jesus had been condemned, Judas his betrayer was filled with remorse and took the thirty silver pieces back to the chief priests and elders. "I have sinned;" he said "I have betrayed innocent blood." "What is that to us?" they replied "That is your concern." And flinging down the silver pieces in the sanctuary he made off, and went and hanged himself. The chief priests picked up the silver pieces and said, "It is against the Law to put this into the treasury; it is blood-money". So they discussed the matter and bought the potter's field with it as a graveyard for foreigners, and this is why the field is called the Field of Blood today. The words of the prophet Jeremiah were then fulfilled: And they took the thirty silver pieces, the sum at which the precious One was priced by children of Israel, and they gave them for the potter's field, just as the Lord directed me. Jesus, then, was brought before the governor, and the governor put to him this question: "Are you the king of the Jews?" Jesus replied, "It is you who say it". But when he was accused by the chief priests and the elders he refused to answer at all. Pilate then said to him, "Do you not hear how many charges they have brought against you?" But to the governor's complete amazement, he offered no reply to any of the charges. (*Mt* 27:1-14; 22-24)

> Pilate said to them "what am I to do with Jesus who is called Christ?" They all said, "Let him be crucified!" "Why?" he asked "What harm has he done?" But they shouted all the louder, "Let him be crucified!" (*Mk* 15:15)

How many pains, how many torments, and how many wounds on the body of Jesus? How much blood falls to the ground, while his tormenters laugh, insult him and gather their strength to hit the innocent body of Jesus again? Let us ask to accept every insult for the love of our Lord, and for true sorrow for our sins.

The Crowning with Thorns

> The governor's soldiers took Jesus with them into the Praetorium and collected the whole cohort round him. Then they stripped him and made him wear a scarlet cloak, and having twisted some thorns into a crown they put this on his head and placed a reed in his right hand. To make fun of him they knelt to him saying, "Hail, king of the Jews!" And they spat on him and took the reed and struck him on the head with it. And when they had finished making fun of him, they took off the cloak and dressed him in his own clothes and led him away to crucify him. (*Mt* 27:27-31)

Think of the indignity, outrage, pain and humiliation that Jesus suffered. They stripped him of every dignity. He was treated as if guilty of our worst sins. He seems to say to us: "Why do you despair when you suffer? Is that the way you love me? Meditate on my passions and find in them great riches." Let us ask for the gift of patience to accept all humiliations, thinking of how Jesus suffered for us.

The Carrying the Cross

> As they were leading him away they seized on a man, Simon from Cyrene, who was coming in from the country, and made him shoulder the cross and carry it behind Jesus. Large numbers of people followed him, and of women too, who mourned and lamented for him. But Jesus turned to them and said, "Daughters of Jerusalem, do not weep for me; weep rather for yourselves and for your children. For the days will surely come when people will say, "Happy are those who are barren, the wombs that have never borne, the breasts that have never suckled!" Then they will begin to say to the mountains, "Fall on us!"; to the hills, "Cover us!" For if men use the green wood like this, what will happen when it is dry? Now with him they were also leading out two other criminals to be executed. (*Lk* 23:26-32)

Even if he had suffered just for you, Jesus would have accepted such pains, so great is his love for you. Along the road to Calvary Jesus sees Mary, his Mother. Can we imagine the moment when their eyes met? Oh how her Heart must have ached. Let us pray to Mary for the grace to always accept our cross.

The Crucifixion and Death of Jesus

Near the cross of Jesus stood his mother's sister, Mary the wife of Clopas, and Mary of Magdala. Seeing his mother and the disciple he loved standing near her, Jesus said to his mother, "Woman, this is your son". Then to the disciple he said, "This is your mother". And from that moment the disciple made a place for her in his home. (*Jn* 19:25-27)

Jesus wishes to see us close to his Mother; he wishes that, like children, we keep our hand in the hand of Mary. That is what he wants. He asks us to look to our heavenly Mother and depend on her. He asks that we accept Our Lady as our true Mother who will ignite in us a fervent love of her Son. Mary, we trust in you, take us and shelter us in your Immaculate Heart, heal with your humility our pride that so often takes us far from God.

Glorious mysteries

The Resurrection of Jesus

After the sabbath, and towards dawn on the first day of the week, Mary of Magdala and the other Mary went to visit the sepulchre. And all at once there was a violent earthquake, for the angel of the Lord, descending from heaven, came and rolled away the stone and sat on it. His face was like lightning, his robe white as snow. The guards were so shaken, so frightened of him, that they were like dead men. But the angel spoke; and he said to the women, "There is no need for you to be afraid. I know you are looking for Jesus, who was crucified. He is not here, for he has risen, as he said he would. Come and see the place where he lay..." (*Mt* 28:1-6)

The risen Jesus has proved that man, together with him, can have power over sin and therefore death. Jesus, help raise us, deliver us from sin, from evil, give us your light, give us your joy. Enkindle in us the love, the faith, the hopefulness and the gift of prayer. Let us ask Mary for the gift of an unshakeable faith.

The Ascension of Jesus

They were still talking about all this when he himself stood among them and said to them, "Peace be with you!" In a state of alarm and fright, they thought they were seeing a ghost. But he said, "Why are you so agitated, and why are these doubts rising in your hearts? Look at my hands and feet; yes, it is I Indeed. Touch me and see for yourselves; a ghost has no flesh and bones as you can see I have." And as he said this he showed them his hands and feet.

"And now I am sending down to you what the Father has promised. Stay in the city then, until you are clothed with the power from on high." Then he took them out as far as the outskirts of Bethany, and lifting

> his hands he blessed them. Now as he blessed them, he withdrew from them and was carried up to heaven. (*Lk* 24:36-40; 49-51)

Jesus, you have not deserted your apostles in anguish, but have given them the joy of knowing Jesus "glorified" over forty days. After your Ascension, you granted to all those who seek you the gift of receiving you in the Eucharist. Through Mary we trust in you. Mary, give us the gift of hope.

The Descent of the Holy Spirit

> When Pentecost day came round, they had all met in one room, when suddenly they heard what sounded like a powerful wind from heaven, the noise of which filled the entire house in which they were sitting; and something appeared to them that seemed like tongues of fire; these separated and came to rest on the head of each of them. They were all filled with the Holy Spirit, and began to speak foreign languages as the Spirit gave them the gift of speech. (*Ac* 2:1-4)

Jesus, infuse us with the Comforter, the Holy Ghost, enlighten us with the light of your Spirit, with his strength enter in the deepest parts of our hearts and heal us. Deliver us, fill up our hearts with your love. Make us apostles of yours, dear Lord. Let us ask Mary for the gift of true love, the gift of prayer from the heart. “Come Holy Spirit, come by means of the powerful intercession of the Immaculate Heart of Mary, your well-beloved Spouse.”

The Assumption of the Virgin Mary

“May you be blessed, my daughter, by God Most High, / beyond all women on earth; / and may the Lord God be blessed, / the Creator of heaven and earth, / by whose guidance you cut off the head / of the leader of our enemies.

“By doing all this with your own hand / you have deserved well of Israel, / and God has approved what you have done.

“May you be blessed by the Lord almighty / in all the days to come!”

All the people answered, “Amen!” (*Jdt* 13:18-20; 15:10)

Now that Mary is raised into heaven, she prays for her sons and daughters, those sons and daughters Jesus left her when he was on the cross. Mary, pray for us, you know our fears, take us into your Heart, the Heart of a Mother. Help us now and in the time of our death to be with you in heaven. We ask of you a devotion to your Immaculate Heart, where we may take refuge in times of trouble.

The Coronation of the Blessed Virgin Mary

> Now a great sign appeared in heaven: a women, adorned with the sun, standing on the moon, and with the twelve stars on her head for a crown. (*Rv* 12:1)

Let us trust in Mary, let us call to her, let us love her, let us confide in her because she gives her all to us. We have a Mother in heaven who is also a queen; thus we need to turn to her full of faith and hopefulness. If we ask for something while praying the Holy Rosary, it will be granted to us. Ask her for the gift of prayer, a prayer of the heart, said only for love, a love for her and Jesus. Let us also ask for a consistency of prayer, to always be joined to her Heart, and therefore to the Heart of Jesus.

Prayers for Consecration

Prayer in preparation for a personal consecration

Sacred Heart of Jesus and Immaculate Heart of Mary, I want to consecrate and commit myself to you personally. Help me in this time of preparation to better understand your extraordinary love for me and to return this love with a deeper life of prayer and a better Christian life. I will gladly pray the Rosary and worship the Blessed Sacrament. I will try to do my best to be more faithful to the Gospel and to the commandments of God and of the Church, especially the commandments to love God and my neighbour. I will participate more actively in the sacrifice of the Mass and observe the first Fridays and Saturdays of each month. Full of trust I seek refuge in the shelter of your loving Hearts. Protect me in all dangers and after my pilgrimage on earth is over, take me to my eternal home in heaven. Amen.

Prayer in preparation for the consecration of a parish

Sacred Heart of Jesus and Immaculate Heart of Mary, our parish wants to consecrate and dedicate itself to you. Help us in this time of preparation to better understand your extraordinary love for us and to return this love with a profound prayer life and a better Christian life. We will gladly pray the Rosary and worship the Blessed Sacrament. We will try our best to be more faithful to the Gospel and the commandments of God and of the Church, especially the commandment to love God and our neighbour. We will participate more actively in the sacrifice of the Mass and observe the first Fridays and Saturdays of each month. Full of trust we seek refuge in the shelter of your loving Hearts. Protect us in all dangers and after our earthly pilgrimage is over, take us to our eternal home in heaven. Amen.

Prayer for the personal consecration of individuals and groups

Eternal Father, in the Holy Spirit I want to consecrate and commit myself to the Hearts of Jesus and Mary and to be a more devoted and faithful child.

Mother Mary, today I (name) commit myself to your Immaculate Heart. Keep me under your maternal protection and lead me to your Son Jesus.

Lord Jesus, through the Immaculate Heart of Mary, I consecrate and commit myself to your Sacred Heart. Mould my heart after your heart so that you will live in me ever more.

Sacred Heart of Jesus and Immaculate Heart of Mary, with this consecration and commitment I return to you the love you showed me in your temporal earthly lives, especially on Calvary, and which you show me still today. At the same time I renew my baptismal consecration to the triune God: I renounce sin, temptation of evil and the devil; I believe in everything that God has revealed to us and which the Catholic Church teaches us.

I promise to fulfil Jesus's commandment of love for God and my neighbour, the commandments of God and of the Church and to act according to the doctrine of the Church under the successor of St Peter. In this way I want to contribute to the unity and growth of the Church. I will personally pray the Rosary with my family and other communities and observe the devotion of the first Fridays and Saturdays, making reparation for my sins and the sins of all mankind.

O Sacred Heart of Jesus and Immaculate Heart of Mary, help me to accept the Gospel in my heart and to live it in faith, hope and love, that Jesus Christ will, through his cross and Resurrection, become the way, the truth and the life for me. May I be nourished on heavenly bread and live out the sacrifice of the Eucharist so that I will overcome every evil and always choose life. Full of trust I seek shelter in your loving Hearts. Protect me in all dangers and after this earthly pilgrimage is over, take me to my eternal home in heaven. Amen.

Prayer for the personal consecration of a family

Jesus, Mary! You lived as a family at Nazareth with Joseph, so every family is dear to you. Mother Mary, the Queen of the family, our family, united in mutual love, commits itself to your Immaculate Heart. Keep us under your maternal protection and lead us to your Son Jesus.

Lord Jesus, gathered in your name through the Immaculate Heart of Mary, we consecrate and commit ourselves to your Sacred Heart. Mould our hearts after your heart so that you will live more and more in us and among us.

Sacred Heart of Jesus and Immaculate Heart of Mary, (families with young children add: we especially consecrate and commit to you the upbringing of our children). Help us to fulfil our duties conscientiously, and to live according to the commandments of God and the Church, especially the commandment to love God and our neighbour, living the Gospel in our hearts and acting according to the teachings of the Church under the leadership of the successor of St Peter. We want to respect one another, forgive one another, faithfully carry our crosses and live a kind of love that is ready to give life for one another. We will not close up in ourselves, but be attentive to the needs of others.

As a domestic Church, our family should be a community of grace and prayer, a school of human and Christian virtues, especially of love. We will gladly co-operate in the life of our parish, participate in Holy Mass and in the Sacrament of Confession, reconciling with God and with one another. The Eucharist shall make us one body. Everyday family and personal prayer shall be our strongest and most powerful encouragement for accepting our responsibilities as a Christian family.

Sacred Heart of Jesus and Immaculate Heart of Mary, protect us from every sin. We resolve especially to avoid sins against faith, hope and love, sins of swearing and unchastity, sins of the tongue and envy, sins of hatred and every evil.

We promise to keep the Lord's Day holy. For the conversion of sinners we will gladly pray the Rosary and observe the devotion of the first Fridays and Saturdays. We will make reparation for all offences that we and the world alienated from God offend you with.

Help us to live constantly in the grace of God and stay faithful to you until the end. May all members of our family reach a happy old age and one day with our friends enjoy eternal happiness in heaven. Amen.

Prayer for the consecration of a parish (1)

(*Singular form*)
Mother Mary, the dawn of our redemption, as a parish priest of (the name of the parish or community) I commit myself and also my parish to your Immaculate Heart. Keep us under your maternal protection and lead us to your Son Jesus, the light of the world, our Redeemer, our hope, and our salvation.

Lord Jesus, through the Immaculate Heart of Mary in the Holy Spirit, I consecrate and commit myself and my parish to your heart. May we be more and more devoted and faithful children of our heavenly Father.

I consecrate and commit to you all the members of this parish, beginning with the weakest ones, from the unborn to the sick, the disabled and the elderly. I commit to you our families, our children, our young people, the single and the widowed. I pray especially for dysfunctional, hurt and broken families, for the young who seek the meaning of life, but who are getting lost in a world of alcohol and drugs. Help the unemployed, the lonely and the desperate. I pray for those who are away from the parish, who have distanced themselves from the Church. Through the intercession of Mary accept all those named in your merciful heart, and make me a co-worker of your mercy.

Merciful Redeemer, increase your grace in us so that we will renew our baptismal consecration to the triune God, renounce sin, the temptation of evil and the devil. We shall believe everything God has revealed to us and which is taught by the Catholic Church. Grant us the Spirit of love so that we will live according to the Gospel, fulfil your commandment to love God and our neighbour, keep the commandments of God and those of the Church, receive sacraments worthily, especially the Sacraments of Reconciliation and the Eucharist and act according to the teachings of the Church. Support us so that we will, in the power of the Holy Spirit with his gifts and charisms, listen to God's call with joy and respond to it generously by co-operating in the new evangelisation, contributing to the unity and growth of the parish and the entire Church.

Encourage us in prayer and grant that we will always feed on the Word of God and heavenly bread. In this way we will be well prepared to overcome every evil and always choose life. Protect us in every danger and take us, through the intercession of our Mother Mary, into the embrace of our merciful heavenly Father after our earthly pilgrimage is over. Amen.

Prayer for the consecration of a parish (2)

(*Plural form*)
Mother Mary, the dawn of our redemption, our parish (name) commits itself to your Immaculate Heart. Accept us under your maternal protection and lead us to your Son Jesus, the light of the world, the only Redeemer, our hope and our salvation.

Lord Jesus, we as a parish consecrate and commit ourselves to your Sacred Heart. May we be ever more devoted and faithful children of our heavenly Father.

We consecrate and commit to you all members of our parish, starting with the weakest ones: from the unborn to the sick, the disabled and the elderly. We commit to you our families, our children, our young people, the single and the widowed. We pray especially for hurting and broken families, and for the young who are searching for meaning in their lives, but who are getting lost in a world of alcohol and drugs. Help the unemployed, the lonely and the desperate. We pray especially for those who have fallen away from the Church, who have distanced themselves from the parish community. Through the intercession of Mary accept all the named in your merciful heart and make us co-workers of your mercy.

Merciful Redeemer, before you we renew our baptismal consecration: we renounce sin, the temptation of evil and the devil. We believe in everything that God has revealed to us and which is taught by the Catholic Church. Grant us the Spirit of love so that we will live according to the Gospel, fulfil your commandment of love for God and our neighbour, the commandments of God and of the Church, receive the sacraments worthily, especially the Sacraments of Reconciliation and the Eucharist, and act in accordance with the doctrine and teachings of the Church. Support us so that we will, in the power of the Holy Spirit with his gifts and charismas, listen to God's call with joy and respond to it generously, co-operating in the new evangelisation, contributing to the unity and growth of the parish and the entire Church.

We want to be nourished on the Word of God and on heavenly bread. We want to pray regularly so that we will be well prepared to conquer every evil and always choose life. Protect us in every danger through the intercession of our Mother Mary, and after our pilgrimage on earth is over, may we be taken into the eternal embrace of our merciful Father in heaven. Amen.

Prayer after the consecration of individuals

Sacred Heart of Jesus, through the Immaculate Heart of Mary, I offer you my thoughts, words and works of this day. Through the intercession of our Mother Mary may my life be in accordance with your Gospel and penetrated with faith, hope and love. Through your cross and Resurrection you will always be the way, the truth and the life for me. Amen.

Prayer after the consecration of a family

Sacred Heart of Jesus and Immaculate Heart of Mary, our family commits and consecrates itself to you with love. Be with us and help us to fulfil Jesus's commandment of love for God and our neighbour, the commandments of God and of the Church and act in accordance with the doctrine and teachings of the Church under the leadership of the successor of St Peter. In this way we will grow in mutual love and unity. Immaculate Heart of Mary, lead us on the way to Jesus! Sacred Heart of Jesus, be our life and Resurrection! Amen.

Prayer after the consecration of a parish

Sacred Heart of Jesus and Immaculate Heart of Mary, our parish commits and offers itself to you entirely. Be with us and help us to fulfil Jesus's commandment of love for God and our neighbour, the commandments of God and of the Church, always acting in accordance with doctrine and teachings of the Church under the leadership of the successor of St Peter. In this way we will grow in mutual love and unity. Immaculate Heart of Mary, lead us on the way to Jesus! Sacred Heart of Jesus, be our life and Resurrection! Amen.

Endnotes

[1] Benedict XVI, *Shepherds of Fatima* (London, Catholic Truth Society, 2010) p. 42.

[2] More information about the consecration is available in the booklet, Fr Anton Nadrah Ocist, *Consecration to the Hearts of Jesus and Mary* (Stična, 2005).

[3] In Portugese the word used is "nasoes", which could also mean "states"; indeed, many states were destroyed, but not nations.

[4] Sister Lucia, *My View on the Message After Some Time and Events Have Passed* (Coimbra, 2007) pp. 52-55.

[5] From the Preliminary Note written by the Bishop of Fatima on 13th October 1997, and published in Sister Lucia's book, *"Calls" from the Message of Fatima* (Postulation Centre in Fatima, 2000) p. 4.

[6] Benedict XVI, *Shepherds of Fatima* (London, Catholic Truth Society, 2010) p. 42.

[7] *http://www.vatican.va/roman_curia/congregations/cfaith/documents/rc_con_cfaith_doc_20000626_message-fatima_en.html*

[8] Tarcisio Bertone, Giuseppe de Carli, *The Last Fatima Seer*, (Klagenfurt, 2008) p. 10. (Foreword, page x, in Cardinal Bertone's book, *The Last Secret of Fatima* (Doubleday, 2008). "Last Secret" is in fact a mistranslation of the Italian title, *L'Ultima Veggente*, or *Last Seer*.)

[9] John Paul II, *Crossing the Threshold of Hope* (Jonathan Cape, 1994) p. 221.

[10] For more on the apparitions at Fatima, see Sister Lucia, *Fatima in Lucia's Own Words* (Postulation Centre for the Causes of Canonisation of Bl. Francisco and Jacinta in Fatima, November 2011) 18th edition.

[11] Ibid., p. 179.

[12] Ibid., p. 177.

[13] Ibid., p. 194.

[14] Ibid., p. 196.

[15] Antonio Maria Martins SJ, *Novos Documentos de Fatima* (Sao Paulo, 1984) p. 258.

[16] Antonio Maria Martins SJ, *O Segredo de Fatima*, p. 170.

[17] Antonio Maria Martins SJ, *Novos Documentos de Fatima* (Sao Paulo, 1984) p. 231.

[18] Antonio Maria Martins SJ, *Novos Documentos de Fatima*, pp. 118-119.

[19] *How I See the Message, in the Course of Time and in the Light of Event*s (published by the Carmel of Coimbra and the Postulation Centre in Fatima, 2006) pp. 38-40.

Picture credits: Page 7: Lúcia Santos, Jacinta and Francisco Marto, 1917, photo attributed to Joshua Benoliel. Page 35: Our Lady of Fatima © Ricardo Perna/Shutterstock.com. Page 44: Basilica of Our Lady of the Rosary, Sanctuary of Fatima, Portugal. © kavramv/Shutterstock.com